All scripture referenc
Version of the Bible, t

Words in capitals, in bold or in Scripture quotations are the emphasis of the author.

The words "him", "his", "he", or "man" are sometimes used generically to describe people of both genders.

Published by PaX Trading Ministries Pty Ltd
Printed in Australia

ISBN No 0 9585827 18

PaX Trading Ministries Pty Ltd
Locked Bag No 8
Dee Why NSW 2099
Australia

Many thanks to:
Amanda Westwood – Editing
Di Payne – Proofing & Finishing

Cover Art & Layout by Velvet Cteative
Printed in Australia by Hyde Park Press

healing
the wounded
spirit

Complete and perfect
healing in Christ

phil pringle

contents

chapter one
healing the wounded spirit

chapter one
healing the wounded spirit

We are spiritual beings. This means we are not just a body. We do not only exist in a physical dimension. We also have a spiritual dimension to our lives. When God formed us, He made us spirit, soul and body.

> *"Now may the God of peace Himself sanctify you completely; and may your whole spirit, soul, and body be preserved blameless at the coming of our Lord Jesus Christ."*
> 1 Thesselonians 5:23

This Scripture tells us we have a spirit, a soul and a body. Body is the physical dimension of our lives. We are in touch with the physical world through our physical senses, touch, taste, sight, smell, and hearing. Our physical being experiences the physical world.

Our soul is that part of us that includes our heart and mind. It is the place of imagination, trust, desire, rhythm, song, art, emotion and dreams. We relate to others and to ourselves with our soul. We experience the heart and emotions of others through our soul. We are creative in our soul. We are 'moved' in our soul by various influences, all of which cause us to behave in a variety of ways (2 Pet 1:21).

Our spirit is the wellspring of our life. It is the basic attitude of our life. It is the seat of motivation. All our life comes from that invisible, mysterious, God conscious area called the spirit. Once the spirit has departed from the body it is dead (James 2:26). Daniel spoke of his spirit in the 'midst' of his body (Dan 7:15). Jesus said that living water flows from the 'innermost being', ('belly', KJV), of believers when they are filled with the Holy Spirit (John 7:38).

Our spirit is that part of us where God dwells after we have received Christ. God communicates with us from deep in our spirit. God is a spirit.

> *"God is Spirit, and those who worship Him must worship in spirit and truth."* John 4:24

If we want to commune with God we must be spiritually alive. Our spirit finds expression through our soul and ultimately through our body.

However, regardless of where and of what substance our spirit is, the Bible continually reveals the high significance of the spirit through countless references to its influence in our lives. When we receive Christ, our spirit is regenerated, that is, it is born again (John 3:3-7).

The complete process of our salvation covers three areas which can be located in three different timings:

i)　　　Our spirit receives complete salvation when we receive Christ (John 1:12). At that point we are born of God (1 John 5:1), who is a spirit (John 4:24). We are born spiritually (John 3:60. This rebirth awakens our spirit to God, and grants to us a 'God awareness'.

ii)　　　Our soul is being saved (1 Cor 1:18), that is, the inner man of our mind is being renewed daily (Rom 12:2). Our emotions, our desires, and trust, our heart, all our being saved as we walk with Christ and feed on the things of God.

iii)　　　Our bodies are not yet saved, but at the resurrection will be (Rom 8:23). Then our redemption will be complete. God shows His guarantee that our salvation will be completed, through filling us with the Holy Spirit (2 Cor 5:4,5), who, when He comes, is accompanied with supernatural phenomena such as speaking in tongues (Acts 10:45, 46).

Even though we have been born again, and have received a 'new spirit' (Ezek 11:19), it appears our spirit is not inviolate from damage. Our spirit can be contaminated with 'filth' (2 Cor 7:1), from which we need to cleanse ourselves. However, one of the most damaging things that can happen to a person's spirit is for them to become spiritually sick. This is when a person's spirit has become damaged and has been left unhealed. The damage becomes infected and that sickness begins to travel throughout their physical and intellectual life, leaving them often confused as to why they are behaving in ways that are out of character.

All of our life springs from our spirit, therefore it is vital we are in good spiritual health. A troubled life can only spring from a troubled fountain, that is an unwell spirit.

> *"Keep your heart with all diligence,*
> *for out of it spring the issues of life."*
> Proverbs 4:23

The word used here, (Hebrew – 'leb'), means 'heart', or the 'centre'. It is referring to the centre of our lives. This needs to be guarded, because our whole life flows from here. The spirit that is wounded causes us to limp through life. There are many Christians who have simply died out on the battlefield and never been revived or raised back to life in Christ.

Just as our physical body needs food and water, our spirit must receive nutrition. Acts 3:19 speaks of 'times of refreshing from the Presence of the Lord'. The word refreshing is added to, and rendered by the Amplified Bible, 'recovery as if from the effects of heat and reviving with fresh air'. However, the upkeep of our spirit is a two-way process and we can choose to let God into our lives or not. It's a choice we make.

2 Kings 4:8 tells the story of a woman who constructs an extra room in her house for

the prophet Elisha. She makes room for God in her life, in her house, in her concepts, in her time, and in her resources. Mary did the same when she accepted that she would be the mother of Jesus. The inn-keeper in Bethlehem failed to 'make room' for God. Making room for God will cost something. Constructing the room for Elisha cost the woman something. For Mary, it was the price of her precious relationship with her fiancee, and then her family, and then her community. For the inn keeper, it was the price of removing some people from their lodgings in order to make room for the young couple.

The woman who constructed the room for Elisha was rewarded with a son, which in itself is miraculous because she has been barren until this point. The child grows and eventually enters the fields to help his father at harvest time. However, the boy becomes sunstruck and in his sick state he is taken to the mother, where he shortly dies. She quickly makes her way to where the prophet currently is and calls on him to help. To help, the prophet sends his servant on ahead, telling him to take Elisha's staff and lay it on the child. However, the prophet's rod in the hand of Gehazi has no effect. In the same way, the successful programs of other successful leaders and preachers will not necessarily be successful in anyone else's hands. Finally Elisha himself arrives and shuts himself alone in the room with the dead boy. He lays upon the lad and stretches himself over the boy again and revives his life. This story is evidence of the powerful effect of revival both to the spirit and the body and of the elements required for such revival.

The only hope for believers whose spirits have died is, only in:

i)   the intercession of other concerned Christians. It is incumbent upon the 'mother', the church, to intercede and bring God to bear upon these people who have simply died.

ii)   a direct encounter with God Himself.

iii)   the Spirit of God reviving them, bring them back to life. This is why it is so imperative for us to allow the Holy Spirit to have His way in our gatherings as Christians, because He alone brings fresh life into the Body of Christ. This is especially true for those slain in the harvest field or in the inevitable battles every Christian faces with the forces of darkness.

However, there are spiritual illnesses that strike at Christians, which are designed to eventually destroy us, leaving us dead. If we are able to deal with, resolve, and heal these illnesses before they cause great damage, we have a far greater chance of enjoying a victorious Christian life. There is healing in Christ. There is always a way through!

sickness of spirit

> *"A wholesome tongue is a tree of life, but perverseness in it breaks the spirit."* Proverbs 15:4

> *"A merry heart does good, like medicine, but a broken spirit dries the bones."* Proverbs 17:22

> *"Then He caused me to pass by them all around, and behold, there were very many in the open valley; and indeed they were very dry."* Ezekiel 37:2

Having no hope, and being dislocated from God and His people had caused dryness in the spirit of the Israelites. This dryness is not superficial. It is a pervasive dryness seeping all the way down into the bones.

Hope is defined as 'the positive anticipation of good'. God is the 'God of hope' (Rom 15:13). Being dislocated from God is being dislocated from the positive anticipation of good. (Eph 2:12, 4:18). In addition, not being with other believers robs us of nourishment God has provided to us through the believers we are surrounded by (Eph 4:16).

Alienation from God and people happens because of offence. Jesus said that offences are unavoidable and inevitable (Luke 17:1). We need to find the ability to recover quickly and completely from these offences. Jesus told us to be 'perfect' as our Father in heaven is perfect (Mat 5:48). Young's Analytical Concordance lists one of the meanings of the word perfect as 'the ability to repair and adjust'. God has never expected that we would attain to a state of life where we never made a mistake, or never offended anyone, nor did any wrong at all. But He does anticipate that we will develop a character that is able to repair breaches.

If repairing is needed in our relationships with others, we must be able to apologise for our part in the offence or forgive those who have caused it. If it is not repairing that is needed, but just a change of purpose, then God wants us to come to a place where we will be mature enough to make adjustments to our purposes. If I have plans that involve others, but the plans are causing unnecessary pressures on them, then I should be able to change enough to allow them to enjoy whatever it is we are attempting together.

The dry bones in the valley were those who had been slain.

> *"…Come from the four winds, O breath, and breathe on these SLAIN, that they may live."* Ezekiel 37:9

The Strongs Hebrew-Greek Concordance indicates the word 'slain', harag, means; 'to smite with deadly intent: ~destroy out of hand, kill, murder put to [death], make [slaughter], slay'. Satan manipulates and deceives in order to ensure that believers become offended and that their wounds remain unhealed. Satan's purpose is to destroy completely. It constantly amazes me

how many of us in the Kingdom of God
live with unresolved offences in our lives.
Unresolved bitterness growing in our spirit
turns everything sour. We are deceived into
thinking no one is good enough. Everyone
is at fault. Our attitudes become negative
and complaining and in this state we find it
extremely difficult to love one another.

Isaiah describes the condition like this;

> *"... The whole head is sick, and the*
> *whole heart faints. From the sole of*
> *the foot even to the head, there is*
> *no soundness in it, but wounds and*
> *bruises and putrefying sores; They*
> *have not been closed or bound up,*
> *Or soothed with ointment."*
> Isaiah 1:5,6

When we are sick in spirit even the drive to
live disappears.

Disappointment is one of the most common
reasons people are sick in their inner man.
The writer of Proverbs says;

"Hope deferred makes the heart sick..." Proverbs 13:12

This disappointment happened to the Hebrews after Moses had announced that God had told him He was going to set the children of Abraham free from the bondage of Pharaoh. Obviously the people became extremely excited. After four hundred years of slavery they hardly dreamed of being free. The prophecies were there, promising hope for the future that a deliverer would come. Now here was Moses, a princely figure, confident of his encounter with God and fully believing that God was about to unshackle the Hebrews. Moses had convinced them he was their deliverer by working miracles which God had shown him with his shepherd's rod. Yet when Moses approached Pharaoh, he was laughed out of the palace.

Even worse, Pharaoh doubled the productivity requirements of the Israelites and provided them with half as much raw material. The situation had only become worse. Much worse. Their expectations had been raised and now were smashed. Disappointed, they were quick to reject Moses, the one responsible for raising their hopes. Incredibly God calls on Moses to return to the elders and restate that God would deliver them. However, because of the wounded state of the Hebrews' hearts they could not hear the message of Moses. He was attempting to being glad tidings to them, but they had no capacity to hear him because their hearts were wounded with heavy disappointment.

> *"So Moses spoke thus to the children of Israel; but they did not heed Moses, because of anguish of spirit and cruel bondage."* Exodus 6:9

Hebrews 4:2 tells us that the Israelites heard the Word, but it did not profit them because it was not mixed with faith. When they heard another promise about deliverance from slavery or of entering the promised land their hearts were too wounded to believe the Word of God.

We live in a generation where people very similar to the disappointed Israelites have great difficulty in even hearing good news because it hurts to believe. It is like an actual pain to lift expectations that have been damaged. Their expectations have been raised and then unfulfilled. So many promises have been made and have not been kept. Therefore trust has been breached. It hurts these people when they have placed on them the spiritual pressure of expecting God to keep His Word. To believe that something good is going to happen because God has said so, is too painful for the spirits of many people. They need the healing hand of Christ to touch their soul, so that cynicism retreats and hope begins to take root again in their lives.

The purpose of the remainder of this book is to discuss the various ways that our Spirit becomes injured and diseased. By recognising these conditions, Christians may be better able to seek God's grace and the guidance of the Holy Spirit to eradicate spiritual disease and to protect against spiritual injury.

the broken spirit

There are two types of broken spirit. There is a brokenness of spirit which is positive and encouraged by Scripture;

> *"The sacrifices of God are a broken spirit, a broken and a contrite heart; These, O God, you will not despise."*
> Psalms 51:17

This psalm refers to the heart that is broken to God. It is speaking of a person who is yielded to the will of God and soft in heart, so that their prime objective is God's purpose rather than their own. These people are repentant and contrite about their sins and come to God broken over their condition. This repentant heart brings a person close to God.

There is another kind of brokenness, however, which is damaging to the soul. This is when a person's spirit and motivation has been broken. These people feel no reason to get up in the morning. They suffer from a mysterious fatigue and generally mild depression. They easily become physically sick. They find faults in others and all the negatives about life are easy to locate. They have an abundance of reasons why they shouldn't bother attempting anything. Life appears hopeless to these people.

Proverbs speaks of this condition in different contexts;

> *"A merry heart makes a cheerful countenance, but by sorrow of the heart the spirit is broken."*
> Proverbs 15:13

> *"A merry heart does good, like medicine, but a broken spirit dries the bones."* Proverbs 17:22

> *"The spirit of a man will sustain him in sickness, but who can bear a broken spirit?"* Proverbs 18:14

These proverbs are saying that even if a person is sick, when their spirit is strong and healthy, they will be able to cope and keep going. But when a person is damaged in their spirit, even the slightest of physical troubles, sickness or otherwise, crushes them.

> *"Whoever has no rule over his own spirit is like a city broken down, without walls."* Proverbs 25:28

This proverb is saying that when we lost control over our spirit, we become defenceless and vulnerable to the attack of the devil. When our spirit is broken, and that damage begins to affect our lives in ways beyond our control, we find ourselves owners of attitudes we wish we didn't have. A damaged spirit becomes impatient and angry. We talk of someone who is 'short of spirit'. This is a person with an unresolved sickness in their soul.

A person becomes broken in spirit when;

1/ Trust is breached.

When our trust is betrayed, our spirit is broken. We place confidence in people with secrets about our life. If we discover that secret has not been kept, trust is breached. We trust when we expect support from another when we're in a battle. If, however, they let us down, fail to support us, or even turn against us, our trust is broken.

A common form of broken trust in today's world is when a partner in marriage is unfaithful. Each partner has security in the fact that both have made a vow, at the deepest level of trust, to remain faithful to one another. This is basis for secure trust. But when that trust is violated through infidelity, the spirit is violently damaged.

God hates divorce because of the spiritual injury it does to people, and to those directly affected, such as children.

> *"...the LORD has been witness between you and the wife of your youth, with whom you have dealt*

treacherously; Yet she is your companion and your wife by covenant." Malachi 2:14

"But did He not make them one, having a remnant of the Spirit? And why one? He seeks godly offspring. Therefore take heed to your spirit, and let none deal treacherously with the wife of his youth."
Malachi 2:15

"For the LORD God of Israel says 'that He hates divorce, for it covers one's garment with violence', says the LORD of hosts. 'Therefore take heed to your spirit, that you do not deal treacherously'." Malachi 2:16

The capacity to trust is a spiritual strength. Our spirit is the reservoir for trust. If trust is broken our spiritual reservoir is depleted and dries up. When dryness sets in, the spirit cracks easily and breaks. If our spirit is broken our ability to trust is broken too.

The shock of betrayal is like us relying on the branch in a tree to support us but it snaps and we fall, breaking the bones in our leg. We can no longer walk properly let alone carry anything heavy. When our spirit is broken, the burden of carrying anything like a burden for others is too great. Often people with a broken spirit are preoccupied with themselves, nurturing the wounds and protecting themselves against ever being betrayed again. While they're in this state their own world means more to them than anyone else.

2/ Failure

Another way a person's spirit can be broken is through an experience of failure. This can leave them with no faith in themselves, or others, or God.

3/ They have had greater responsibility than they could bear.

Some people have been promoted beyond their competency or their capacity. Even though it may be flattering to be considered better than we really are, eventually the load on our spirit will break us just like a 'too heavy' load on someone will break their bones.

4/ They have carried the responsibility for something which they did not have commensurate authority for.

This situation is one sure way to break a person's spirit. I once met a man who had been made Pastor of a church while the previous minister was away. The previous minister had actually fallen into immorality with a woman and was sent away to recover in another church, under the minister of that congregation. My friend had been given the responsibility, but was told he was not to make any decisions regarding the church. He had the responsibility but no authority. So if he encountered a problem, he would be responsible for it, but have no power to rectify it. He found the situation impossible, and had to leave.

We know we've been broken in spirit when we have lost initiative and motivation; when we lost creative urge; when even sunny days look bleak; when depression and discouragement come easily; when we find it painful to be encouraged or raise faith that God will do good; when we are continually suspicious of everyone, even our closest friends; when we're feeling exhausted for no real reason, and when we react badly to people placing pressure on us for decisions or help of some sort.

The parallels between physical sickness and spiritual sickness are very close, and the healing processes employed for physical problems are similar in concept to those that bring healing to a person's spirit.

Fortunately, when a bone has been broken, it will heal, however it requires nutrients and special conditions for it to heal properly. The bone must be aligned correctly and supported so that undue load is removed. If the bone is not aligned correctly it may heal, but be out of normal alignment and this causes abnormal posture and then deformity throughout the body. In addition, the blood supply to the bone must be intact so nutrients can be taken to the healing bone.

Likewise, all loads should be taken off the person who has been seriously broken in spirit. Just like a person continuing to carry a physically heavy weight with a broken limb, the burden of continuing to carry responsibility will cause great pain to the spirit that is broken. The person will not enjoy carrying out their job. They need to be removed from responsibility for a short period. The seriousness of the break needs to be recognised so that it can be determined how much of a burden should be removed and how long the person should be relieved.

Often people do not withdraw and allow themselves time to heal, and under the pressure of continuing to bear the load, they actually do heal, but in a very disfigured way. It seems to me that there are some experiences people go through in the Lord where He has to literally break the bones that have set wrongly so they can be reset properly and heal correctly. The most common process causing a bad mend is when people adopt a cynical, untrusting, defence system, by which people and love are prevented from entering their lives. This blockage is similar to blocking an artery to the bone, as it prevents essential nutrition from entering a person's spirit. The emotional nourishment that comes from intimate relationships is cut off and the person just starves in those areas of their life.

The person should be surrounded by strong supportive people (like a cast on a broken bone) who will help them carry out the normal responsibilities of life. They should also enter a time of confinement (like hospitalisation). This involves activating a greater set of disciplines in the sufferer's life for a period whilst they heal – the discipline of prayer and Bible reading, restraint from things that are questionable in their

Christian life. This environment speeds up the restoration of a broken spirit.

chapter two
lacerations of the spirit

chapter two
lacerations of the spirit

When a person is lacerated or 'cut' in their spirit, they bleed black, angry, thoughts and ugly emotions. We are cut when people use sharp words that are intended to wound us. Scripture speaks of these people;

> *"My soul is among lions; I lie among the sons of men who are set on fire, whose teeth are spears and arrows, and their tongue a sharp sword."*
> Psalms 57:4

"Who sharpen their tongue like a sword, and bend their bows to shoot their arrows; bitter words…"
Psalms 64:3

"There is one who speaks like the piercings of a sword, but the tongue of the wise promotes health."
Proverbs 12:18

"There is a generation whose teeth are like swords, and whose fangs are like knives, to devour the poor from off the earth, and the needy from among men." Proverbs 30:14

When we are cut in our flesh the wound has to be cleansed so it doesn't become infected. It needs to be bandaged so it is protected and can heal without interruption. Whether the cut is deep or superficial it needs to be closed somehow, either by stitching it together or by drawing it together with a bandage.

We close the cut in our spirit by forgiving and forgetting. It can be an extremely difficult thing to let go of unkind words, unfair treatment, and actions that have wounded our spirit. These offences seem to resurface time and again in our memories causing the same pain to be relived over and over. If we desire to be free from this hurt, it is imperative that we forgive whoever caused the wound and forget their words and their actions. Frequently, these memories are more painful to the spirit than the actual offending events. We should also learn from the experience how to arrange our relationship with the person involved in a way that does not facilitate the offensive behaviour in the future. We cannot afford to keep reopening the wound.

It is often more difficult to forget than it is to remember. Some people complain of having a poor memory. They forget things and cannot remember others. On the contrary, an even bigger problem is having a mind that continually remembers things it should forget.

"Do not remember the former things, nor consider the things of old." Isaiah 43:18

" 'I, even I, am He who blots out your transgressions for My own sake; And I will not remember your sins.' " Isaiah 43:25

"State your case, that you may be acquitted." Isaiah 43:26

Jesus has told us that if we are to expect forgiveness from God it is dependant upon us being forgiving towards those who have wronged us.

"... and forgive us our sins, as we forgive those who sin against us." Matthew 6:12

Jesus placed this request in the Lord's Prayer, so He considered forgiveness to be very important in our spiritual lives.

Forgiveness is the key to healing.

> *"Who forgives all your iniquities,*
> *who heals all your diseases ..."*
> Psalms 103:3

The two forms of healing, both physical and spiritual are often linked together in Scripture:

> *"For which is easier, to say, 'Your sins*
> *are forgiven you', or to say, 'Arise and*
> *walk'?"* Matthew 9:5

Forgiveness applies equally to the healing processes of the soul. Even in the act of forgiving someone, healing flows into the victim's heart. The relationship is healed, and the offender will also experience healing from rejection.

The art of forgiveness must be learned, because every one of us will suffer offences throughout our lives. To forgive is to stand in the presence of God in prayer, and say, 'I forgive so and so. I bless them in the Name of Jesus'. Jesus said we must do this, 'from the heart'. So this is not some superstitious ritual, but the heartfelt actual forgiveness of an offending person. It is ripping up any IOU's. It is being able to state that there is not a soul on Earth that you are holding any grudge against. Not a soul on Earth owes you a thing in the way of an apology.

Understand that forgiveness precedes the offenders repentance. We don't wait for them to approach us with an apology before we forgive them. Rather, we forgive them before they ever make the approach. In fact, it is likely that they are far less likely to approach you with any apology if you have a resentful, condemning attitude. However, people repent and admit to wrongdoing more easily in an environment of forgiveness and acceptance than of condemnation and rejection.

Many people feel that they are at the mercy of their own thoughts and emotions. They believe they have little or no control over what they think or feel. However, we can prevent our lives from being hijacked by these areas. We all have the capacity to control our thoughts and our emotions. Jesus said:

> *"Let not your heart be troubled; you believe in God, believe also in Me."*
> John 14:1

This means we are to disallow our hearts from being troubled. We can stop anxiety from ruling our emotions. The ways of preventing anxiety are found in God's Word.

First we must learn to speak the Word of God. When we confess the promises of God's Word, our faith is built up (Rom 10:17), and the devil is defeated through the sharp, two edged sword of the Spirit (Eph 6:17).

Second, we must discipline our thoughts to remain on those things that create faith and peace, and stop our mind from dwelling on things that depress us. This discipline of thinking can seem like a Herculean effort for some. It seems impossible, but it isn't.

> *"Finally, brethren, whatever things are true, whatever things are noble, whatever things are just, whatever things are pure, whatever things are lovely, whatever things are of good report, if there is any virtue and if there is anything praiseworthy; meditate on these things."* Philippians 4:8

> *"... casting down arguments and every high thing that exalts itself against the knowledge of God, bringing every thought into captivity to the obedience of Christ ..."*
> 2 Corinthians 10:5

As we close the wound on the past, healing flows easily. As people heal from being cut in their spirit, they must not fellowship with those who are negative and bitter. They must surround themselves with positive spiritually healthy people. This environment, plus worship, acts like an antiseptic so they do not become infected. The strange thing is, so many wounded people seek out others unhealthy just like them and consolidate their state rather than healing being able to take place. We must resist the temptation to feed our hurts, but rather we take the medicine that will bring healing.

chapter three
the bruised spirit

chapter three
the bruised spirit

Jesus said, he had come to heal those who were 'bruised' (crushed, smitten through, shattered, broken by calamity). People experience all kinds of crushing experiences through life. These experiences are blunt, unexpected, sudden calamities, that leave us dazed and bruised. Just like when we are bruised on our arm, we become sensitive to any pressure being placed on it. Again, people with a bruised spirit become impatient, intolerant, and short of spirit. Time is the best environment for healing the bruised heart. Blunt tactless words leave people bruised as well. Many artists of one kind or another who bravely step out to present their talent find themselves assailed by critics from every angle. Often these people just shrink away, never to recover. Many preachers find themselves under all kinds of attack for standing up for Christ. Virtually always the attack is not focused on Jesus but on things that are personal to the minister. I've seen preachers just fall out of the race, simply because they could not take the onslaught any more. Someone said they felt that Charles Spurgeon died at an early age, in his fifties, because of the depression from the constant criticisms the press brought against him. Recovering from a bruising is important.

Jesus said He had come to heal those who were bruised or crushed in this life. In fact Isaiah spoke of Jesus as the one who:

> *"A bruised reed He will not break,*
> *and smoking flax He will not quench;*
> *He will bring forth justice for truth."*
> Isaiah 42:3

This verse means there are those who after going through a crushing experience find themselves unable to really get up and get going again. Their fire has gone out. They are a smouldering wick – they're a 'bruised reed'. Feeling useless causes these people to feel that God has no use for them either, and it may be normal to expect that God would just break off a bruised reed or snuff out the smoking flax. But this is not the case. Jesus strengthens the bruised reed so it will be useful, and sets a fire to the smoking flax so it ignites into flame again. He revives passion to the limp heart, and strength to the spirit that is bent over.

In fact we are told that Jesus himself was 'bruised' on our behalf, and took our grief upon himself;

> *"But He was wounded for our transgressions, He was bruised for our iniquities; The chastisement for our peace was upon Him, and by His stripes we are healed."* Isaiah 53:5

Simply understanding why we are like we are, can help the healing process so that we are made whole again as quickly as possible from the inevitable bruises life deals out.

Every relationship we're involved in will need effort to make it work. There will be times when the relationships we have are difficult and even seem to fall apart.

If we react wrongly to the demands our relationships place upon us, we will find people just responding badly to us and we end up with even more bruising. One of the best experiences on earth is to find ourselves not reacting in a negative way like we used to in the same situations. We know then we're healed. We know then we've grown, and we are stronger.

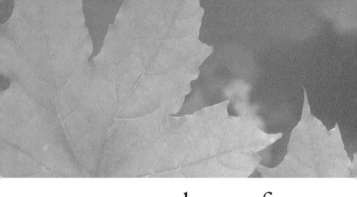

chapter four
the poisoned spirit

chapter four
the poisoned spirit

"They sharpen their tongues like a serpent; The poison of asps is under their lips." Selah Psalms 140:3

One of the saddest things I've experienced is knowing good people who've turned bad. Unfortunately the devil gets into people's attitude and they turn from being the sweetest of saints into bitter, accusative, revengeful people.

The Bible warns against the impact of unresolved bitterness.

> *"...looking carefully lest anyone fall short of the grace of God; lest any root of bitterness springing up cause trouble, and by this many become defiled ..."* Hebrews 12:15

This root of bitterness is a poison that is imparted from one person to another simply through gossip and unnecessarily critical conversation. It is so easy to become poisoned in your view of another person, simply through listening to the backbiting tongue of someone who dislikes them.

Do not entertain anyone who seeks to poison you against another with their conversation. Those who manipulate relationships in this way eventually become poisoned in their attitude to life all around.

> *"The north wind driveth away rain: so doth an angry countenance a backbiting tongue."* Proverbs 25:23

This poison of gossip about others can be directed straight at us also. I've received letters occasionally that have a bad spirit in them. As I read, the spiritual poison starts to come through the words. Suddenly all kinds of negative emotions and trouble thoughts arise.

The means of getting rid of this poison are:

1/ Feed on the Word of God;

> *"You are already clean because of the word which I have spoken to you."*
> John 15:3

2/ Let the Holy Spirit wash through you in worship;

> *"... not by works of righteousness which we have done, but according to His mercy He saved us, through the washing of regeneration and renewing of the Holy Spirit ..."*
> Titus 3:4

3/ Fellowship with other good, strong positive believers this brings cleansing;

> *"But if we walk in the light as He is in the light, we have fellowship with one another, and the blood of Jesus Christ His Son cleanses us from all sin."* 1 John 1:7

Rejection and disappointment are two of the major culprits for causing a poisoned spirit.

Both Jesus and Paul understood the need for people who were receiving rejection to experience the opposite, both from people and God, if they were to be healed and restored.

After Peter had denied Christ three times, (just as Jesus said, 'before the cock crows'), he told the others he was going 'fishing'. This was a return to his previous life. He was on a backward journey. His heart had been so disappointed in himself, and in Christ. He had previously had every confidence that he would easily eclipse the devotion of the other disciples under pressure. He was sure he would never deny Christ. He had even announced his superiority of commitment to Jesus in front of the other disciples;

> *"Peter declared, 'If everyone else deserts you, I won't.'"*
> Matthew 26:33

> *"Jesus told him, 'The truth is that this very night, before the cock crows at dawn, you will deny me three times!'"* Matthew 26:34

We set ourselves up for a fall as soon as we become conceited in our opinion of ourselves. Prov 26:12 says there's more hope for a fool than for someone who is 'wise in their own eyes', (i.e. conceited).

We also set ourselves up for disappointment when we have expectations on ourselves that are too high. Expectations can come from:

- What others expect of us.
- What we imagine others expect of us.

- What we think God requires of us.
- What we expect of ourself.

Peter had failed Jesus, and himself, and the others. They were all discouraged over their seemingly fickle commitment. Not one had seemed to remain as true as they would have liked. Yet the Healer of the broken heart knew that Peter needed some attention. This wound to his spirit needed to be resolved. When the angel gave the message about the resurrection to the women first at the tomb, he made special mention of Peter:

> " 'But go, tell His disciples; and Peter; that He is going before you into Galilee; there you will see Him, as He said to you.' " Mark 16:7

Then when Jesus appears to the disciples on the shore, he exposes the wound and then heals it by asking Peter if he really does love Him (more than the other disciples). He asks him three times, and each time reassures Peter of His love for him, and his acceptance with God, and that a great purpose still awaits him (John 21:15 ...). On the third time, it is inevitable that Peter would be reminded of the fact that he denied Jesus the same number. When the interview was finished Peter was healed. Yet this was not what we could call a supernatural, miraculous healing. It was the healing that happens when we know we have failed, yet we are still loved and accepted by God. This in turn helps us to accept and love ourselves in a healthy way.

Paul had led the Corinthian church through a disciplining process. A certain brother had been involved in sexual deviations (not even named among the heathen). Paul had instructed the church to expel him. Yet, in his second letter, Paul sends the message that they should receive him back into the church so that he would not be destroyed by the depression of rejection;

> *"... so that, on the contrary, you ought rather to forgive and comfort him, lest perhaps such a one be*

swallowed up with too much sorrow.
Therefore I urge you to reaffirm your
love to him." 2 Corinthians 2:7,8

Rejection is a wound that must be healed. Believing the Word of God will bring us to the healing realisation that God has accepted us. Fellowshipping with people that do accept us will bring healing as well.

two very different men
Joseph and Gideon

two very different men
Joseph and Gideon

The Old Testament offers the stories of two men who both enjoyed great success but also suffered terrible wounds to their soul. One resolved his problem and the other didn't. The fruit of their lives bears out the high importance of dealing with the wounded spirit.

Joseph

The young seventeen year old boy Joseph receives two dreams from God telling him that he would one day rule, and not just rule over a nation, but rule over his own family too. Because Joseph was the last and youngest son of Jacob and Rachel, he enjoyed a favouritism over all his brothers. His father had indicated his pleasure in this young son of his old age, by making him a special multicoloured coat (Gen 37:3). The brothers did not appreciate all this favour shown towards this young upstart, and then to increase their jealous hatred, he comes up with these dreams! As if they were simply going to sit by and imagine that Joseph would rule over them. They set out to actually kill their younger brother. Reuben intercedes for him and says, rather than killing him they should sell him as a slave (Gen 37:21).

So Joseph is sold as a slave into the service of a man called Potiphar in Egypt. He serves so well, he is made the overseer of the man's entire household. The household prospers. However, Joseph is evidently a very desirable young man, especially to the wife of Potiphar. She pursues him daily. He resists all her advances, until finally one day she makes a grab for him, but he flees, leaving her with his coat in her hand. The woman, furious with rejection, accuses Joseph of attempting to rape her and he is thrown into prison.

Again he rises to become the warden of the prison, and again whatever is under his command prospers. Two men have dreams which Joseph interprets for them. He asks to be remembered once they are free. They are both released, but neither of them remember Joseph to the King. About two years later, the King himself has a dream and cannot understand it. The butler, who himself had once been in prison, remembers Joseph's ability to interpret dreams and the King summons the prisoner.

Joseph reveals the meanings of the dreams clearly and so the king immediately confers upon Joseph the Presidency under himself of the entire land of Egypt, second only to Pharaoh.

The message of the series of dreams was that seven years of great prosperity would come upon Egypt, which would be followed by seven years of famine and drought. In light of this Joseph had offered counsel that the King should store up provisions in the seven years of prosperity so that he would be able not only to survive the seven years of famine but also have grain to sell to other nations during the famine.

All this came to pass, and when the years of famine did come, Joseph's family was amongst those who were affected. They, like everyone else surrounding Egypt, eventually came to seek supplies for their own survival. When Joseph saw his brothers, bowing down before him, the dream he had received from the Lord when he was a child was finally coming to pass. He remains disguised from his brothers until he has ensured that the entire family, including his father, is before him in Egypt. Because Joseph has held onto his dream and maintained a pure heart he is not at this stage wanting to exact any revenge. In fact, he commands everyone else to leave his presence and he weeps and weeps and weeps. Right then his heart is healed of the wounds of rejection and betrayal he had experienced at the hands of his own brothers. He explains to them that what they meant for evil God meant for good.

Jesus has told us that the pure in heart will blessed for they shall see God (Mat 5:8). When our hearts are clean we can see God in whatever happens to us. Rather than growing bitter we grow better. Vision for our lives has a lot to do with a clean heart. The apostle John said that when our hearts are filled with hatred we are blind, unable to see, walking in darkness (1 John 2:11). Joseph continued to prosper, as did his family with him and after him. He was able to bring his father and brothers and all their families with them into the choicest land of Egypt. The fruit of a person's heart that remains right before the Lord will always be good. This is really what we are attempting to say in this book. It is vital that our heart is healthy, because our whole life springs from that well, and those that we influence and lead. We will either be part of the answer in this world or a part of the problem.

Gideon

The Canaanite tribe of the Midianites has been oppressing the Israelites for several years, trampling their harvests, stealing their animals, and threatening life itself, all as part of God's judgement against the unlearning Hebrews. Fresh sins brought new judgements. A prophet announces that God will raise up a deliverer in responses to the cries for help from the people. An angel appears to Gideon, who is threshing wheat at the time. He is, however, threshing in a wine press, hidden from the view of the Midianites. Although fearful, at least he is doing something. The angel addresses him as a 'mighty man of valour' and continues to tell him 'the Lord is with you!' Gideon is passionate and cynical in his reply, revealing his disappointment, maybe even anger with God. He is carrying a wound in his soul which now has opportunity to be healed as his destiny also unfolds. Gideon retorts, " '...if the LORD is with us, then why has all this happened to us? And where are all His miracles which our fathers told us about, saying, 'Did not the LORD bring us up from Egypt?' But now the LORD has forsaken us and delivered us into the hands of the Midianites." (Judg 6:13)

The angel instructs Gideon to go and tear down the altar of Baal in the town and then to gather Israel to fight against the enemy. He immediately erects an altar to the Lord as an act of worship, but also in superstitious fear that he needed to somehow atone for the fact that he had seen God and would now die. Gideon sneaks into the town square in the middle of the night and dismantles the altar to Baal. Again, his fears and doubts surface. In fact, almost every step of the way Gideon is shown as a person without a lot of confidence, faith in God or even courage. He then seeks confirmation that it really is

God that is calling him to the task, by placing a fleece out for two nights asking God to place dew on the ground but not on the fleece one night and then vice versa the next. The story shows how eager the Lord Himself was to encourage and confirm Gideon. Yet Gideon still fails to learn the lesson. Once the warriors of Israel are gathered, the Lord tells Gideon there are too many. The army is whittled down to a mere three hundred men. This has Gideon in a spin. He wonders how on earth he will ever be able to overwhelm the hordes of Midianites with this tiny band of men he is left with. God gives the man a strategy, so that he stands by night completely surrounding the camp with his men. They are each holding a lamp and a trumpet in their hands. At a shout from their commander, they let the light of the lamps shine and blast on their trumpets. In the confusion that followed, the enemy began to slay one another, not knowing who the attackers were.

After this, Gideon and his men pursue the nomads all the way to Jordan. Men from the other tribes of Israel came, joining the pursuit and reclaiming their lands. When Gideon and his three hundred men came to Jordan they were exhausted and hungry. Amazingly, by this time about 120,000 enemy soldiers had been slain in the battle, with about 15,000 remaining (Judg 8:10). Gideon asked the local inhabitants of Succoth and Penuel for refreshments and food for his men. They refused, on the basis that they had not yet accomplished a complete victory. Gideon promises a punishment on them for their lack of faith in him. Even though God had been gracious to Gideon all the way through the process, now Gideon was not willing to grant the same mercy to these people.

Had Gideon always been completely assured of his victory maybe he would have appeared a little more justified in this attitude, but seeing as he himself had had difficulty in believing, maybe he could have shown more mercy at this point. Once he had overwhelmed the enemy and captured their Kings, he returned to the two towns and killed the men of Penuel and whipped the elders of Succoth with thorns from the wilderness. This act of cruel revenge was something the sweet psalmist of Israel (David), would never have done. On the days of his victories, not even those who had betrayed him were punished. It was to be a day of grace, joy and celebration, not a time for exactly revenge and retribution. Not even King Saul who seems to live with a very insecure soul, wounded with inferiority, seeks revenge on a day of salvation (1 Sam 11:13). However, Gideon acted in this way because of an unresolved, open wound in his soul.

The people of Israel ask Gideon to become their King. He defers becoming their King, declaring that it should be the Lord that rules over them, but he does take up the position of a leader, and immediately takes gold earrings which was spoil from the Ishmaelites and after melting it down makes a gold ephod from it. It becomes an object of worship and the children of Israel 'played the harlot' with it from then on. It became a snare to Israel and the family of Gideon. He also had many wives and many children, 70 sons in fact. After Gideon died, his cruelty revisited him, and all his sons but one were killed in a quest for the throne by one of his sons, Abimelech.

The need therefore for a spirit that is healed and whole is paramount.

The only One who can heal us on the inside completely and perfectly is Christ. And He has promised to do just that. All he needs from us is our willingness to cooperate. We do this by asking Jesus to come into our lives. We ask for forgiveness and cleansing. We repent from our sins, confess them and decide to turn from them. We commit our lives to Christ and begin to live out that commitment by reading the Bible and praying daily, and then fellowshipping and worshipping with other believers in a congregation we feel comfortable in. This great new life begins by being born again. If you have never been born again, then pray this prayer;

Dear God,

I ask Jesus Christ to come into my life.
I receive Him as my Saviour.
I ask to be born again.
I ask to be cleansed from all my sin.
I repent and ask You to forgive me.
I commit my life to You Lord.
In the Name of Jesus.
Amen.

If this is the first time you have prayed this prayer or you are returning to the Lord and making a fresh commitment to Him, please write to us at the address below so we are able to help you in following Christ.

Dr. Phil Pringle

Christian City Church, Oxford Falls
Locked Bag No 8
DEE WHY NSW 2099
AUSTRALIA

If you enjoyed

healing the wounded spirit

**we would like to recommend the following
books by Dr Phil Pringle.**

Faith
Moving in The Spirit And The Anointing
Dead For Nothing
You The Leader
Keys To Financial Excellence
The Leadership Files

Also by Chris Pringle.

Jesse - Found in Heaven

For more information please write to:

PaX Ministries Pty Ltd
Locked Bag 8, Dee Why
NSW 2099 AUSTRALIA
Email: pax@ccc.org.au

or visit the Pax website at
www.ccc.org.au/pax

GAIN...
Enthusiasm, opportunity, significance, focus,
success, passion, patience, wisdom...

DEAL WITH...
Discouragement, culture, people, attitudes, criticism
unfinished business, guilt, confrontation...

'THE LEADERSHIP FILES' series is a compilation of notes t
YOU the LEADER, giving you quick, practical, encouraging
and inspiring messages that will assist you in the day-to-d
issues of life and leadership. Your world will transform as
you apply these to your daily life.

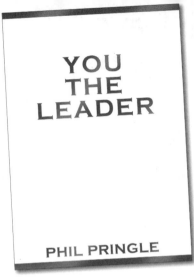

What people are saying about "You The Leader" by Dr Phil Pringle

"I would like to recommend 'You the Leader' by Dr. Phil Pringle. All true Christians are called to use their talents and gifts in a position of authority in the Body of Christ. This book will help each Christian understand his or her role in the Body of Christ."

Dr. David Yonggi Cho
The Yoido Full Gospel Church, Seoul, Korea

"Phil Pringle is an apostolic leader par-excellence. He is also one of the few leaders who knows how to mentor others and to communicate what he knows. 'You The Leader', is crammed full of extraordinary insights that will help you become the dynamic leader that God wants you to be! I highly recommend it."

C. Peter Wagner, Chancellor
Chancellor, Wagner Leadership Institute, USA

"'You The Leader' is a must read for any person who feels called to leadership in the body of Christ. Dr Pringle's insight, gained from over 30 years of pastoral ministry, is practical, biblically based and include thinking in the area of leadership that I believe to be revolutionary in the contemporary church"

Joyce Meyer
Joyce Meyer Ministries, St. Louis, USA

"Safe in angels arms,
far from here,
our children run and play..."

"Jesse...Found in Heaven" will bring hope and comfort to every family suffering the loss of a baby or child.

"
What a beautiful treasure this book has been in my life and the lives of those I have shared it with. 'Jesse – Found In Heaven' has touched a place deep in my heart personally and has created a greater anticipation for the wonder and beauty of what we will encounter when we are reunited with our little loved ones in Heaven. What joy! **"**

Helen Burns
Senior Pastor Victory Christian Centre, Vancouver BC
TV Presenter "Pure Sex and Relationships"
CH 10 Vancouver BC

Video and Audio
CD also available.